The Five Building Blocks of
Success

Other Books by David A. Bragen

A BEGINNER'S GUIDE TO A SUCCESSFUL CAREER

ForeWord Magazine awarded a Gold Medal in the Career category to *A Beginner's Guide to a Successful Career* in its Sixth Annual Book of the Year Awards program. *A Beginner's Guide to a Successful Career* is available online at Amazon.com and Booksamillion.com.

Excerpt from letter to David A. Bragen from Susan Driscoll, President and CEO of iUniverse:

"This year's competition yielded a record-breaking number of 1,500 entries. A Beginner's Guide to a Successful Career looks like a wonderfully practical guide for those entering the work force (in fact, I'm ordering one for my son!) and I'm delighted that it has now been recognized as one of the finest independently published books ..."

CORPORATE CHARACTERS

Understanding the Personalities of Your Co-Workers

iUniverse has awarded both an Editor's Choice (October 2006) and Publisher's Choice designation to *Corporate Characters* (November 2006). *Corporate Characters—Understanding the Personalities of Your Co-Workers* is available online at Amazon.com and Booksamillion.com.

Excerpt from letter to David A. Bragen from Susan Driscoll, President and CEO of iUniverse.… .

"Congratulations! iUniverse has awarded your book Corporate Characters *with the Publisher's Choice designation … designates your book as a high-quality work both inside and out …"*

The Five Building Blocks of

Success

Getting Your Business Career Started on the Right Track and Keeping It There

David A. Bragen

Author of *A Beginner's Guide to a Successful Career*
and *Corporate Characters: Understanding the
Personalities of Your Co-Workers*

iUniverse, Inc.
New York   Lincoln   Shanghai

The Five Building Blocks of Success
Getting Your Business Career Started
on the Right Track and Keeping It There

Copyright © 2007 by David A. Bragen

iUniverse books may be ordered through booksellers or by contacting:

iUniverse
2021 Pine Lake Road, Suite 100
Lincoln, NE 68512
www.iuniverse.com
1-800-Authors (1-800-288-4677)

Because of the dynamic nature of the Internet, any Web addresses or links contained in this book may have changed since publication and may no longer be valid.

The views expressed in this work are solely those of the author and do not necessarily reflect the views of the publisher, and the publisher hereby disclaims any responsibility for them.

ISBN: 978-0-595-43359-9 (pbk)
ISBN: 978-0-595-87685-3 (ebk)

Printed in the United States of America

Contents

Preface

The Five Building Blocks of Success—Getting Your Business Career Started on the Right Track and Keeping It There describes the five key components that you must master to achieve success at work. We will take an in-depth look at the critical success factors that will assist you in achieving your goals. Ultimately, as you will see as you progress through this text, your success is dependent upon your own efforts and performance in the roles that you will encounter during your career. This book is designed to bring a number of important issues to the forefront so that you can expand your thinking and, through that effort, increase your level of performance.

During my career, which has spanned over thirty years, I have worked with many successful people and, at times, have achieved high levels of success of my own. I have also encountered a number of supposedly successful people who did not seem to be making much of a job-related contribution. This text will examine what makes the successful people successful.

As a member of various senior managements over the years, I have had the pleasure of promoting numerous individuals. I have also faced the unpleasant task of firing many people. What separates the two groups? Why do some succeed while others fail? What does management look for in its employees in an attempt to determine who has the right stuff? I will answer all of these questions in *The Five Building Blocks of Success—Getting Your Business Career Started on the Right Track and Keeping It There.*

Prior to becoming a consultant and assisting other companies in various areas, I was the president of a division of a multi-billion-dollar company. Together with the vice president of human resources, I crafted a developmental program for high-potential employees to ensure that we would have a continuous stream of talented employees poised for promotion. I am proud to say that, of the twenty-four individuals who comprised the first two classes, twenty-one received promotions within the first two years of completing the developmental program. All of these individuals possessed all five of the building blocks addressed in this book. Over time, these strengths became the basis for the model I developed to identify high-potential individuals, and also to provide general guidance to my entire group as to what "management" was looking for from employees.

Your career is a journey that will not end until your last day of work. In my first book, *A Beginners Guide to a Successful Career*, I addressed topics such as selecting a company to work for, developing positive work habits, learning how to work effectively as part of a team, learning the basics of sales to assist you in securing what you want, and understanding the role of supervisor after your first promotion. In my second book, *Corporate Characters—Understanding the Personalities of Your Co-Workers*, I explored the makeup and characteristics of a number of personality types that you would encounter throughout your career. In both books I introduced tips, guidelines, and strategies to assist you in the continuous improvement process that will become your career.

The Five Building Blocks of Success—Getting Your Business Career Started on the Right Track and Keeping It There completes the trilogy that will enable you to be best positioned for future career success.

Introduction

A new Rolex watch, a mint-condition '87 Buick Grand National capable of going from 0 to 60 mph in 5.2 seconds, a summer home in southwestern Michigan, a closet full of designer suits, and financial security—these are some of the trappings of success.

A well-deserved raise, a promotion, an assignment to a high-powered team, the respect and admiration of your peers—these are also some of the trappings of success.

Ask ten different people how they measure success and you will most likely receive ten different answers. Ask those same ten people how they define success and you will see some variation in their answers as well.

Defining success by the material things that accrue to the successful is a shortsighted and simplistic assessment of a very complicated concept. Defining success in terms of its impact on others as well as the organizations we come into contact with is a more meaningful representation of the concept. Yet even this approach, measuring success as seen through the eyes of others, is somewhat ambiguous and arbitrary. Often, while two people make the same contribution, only one of them is heralded as a success, while the other is seen as average. Defining success through the eyes of others introduces some distracting and inescapable side issues such as office politics, personality differences, and plain, old-fashioned individual biases.

For the purposes of the journey we are about to undertake, we will look at success through the eyes of the individual. You, and only you, can truly define what constitutes success as it applies to your own contributions to the greater good of the organization in which you work. This approach, however, does not lessen the hurdles that need to be overcome to truly be successful, neither does it suggest that your own definition can somehow make attainment easier.

Ultimately, if you are truly successful, even within the reasonable but meaningful parameters you have established for yourself, others will recognize that success.

Another important distinction of success is that it does not guarantee that you will receive the material rewards normally associated with success, or the glowing accolades of your peers. We all recognize that sometimes success is not recognized for a variety of reasons including, but not limited to, jealousy and covetousness. Yet, these reasons should not stop us from striving to achieve success for, in addition to the material rewards and glowing accolades, success can also result in the inner recognition of a job well done.

As we continue this journey I will establish four basic assumptions, which will form the foundation of *The Five Building Blocks of Success—Getting Your Business Career Started on the Right Track and Keeping It There*. These assumptions are:

1. You have a true desire to become and remain successful.

2. You understand and accept that success is fleeting if the effort is not maintained.

3. Your primary measurement of success is the inner recognition of a job well done, and not the material rewards or glowing accolades heaped upon the successful.

4. You realize that hard work and dedication in accomplishing your organizational responsibilities is the starting point upon which a successful career can be built.

The last item I will cover before we briefly introduce The Five Building Blocks of Success is the fact that most of us really do want the Rolex, the Grand National, and the vacation house in southwestern Michigan. We want the raises, promotions, and personal accolades that come to successful people in commercial enterprises. There is nothing intrinsically wrong with these wants and desires. But you must also recognize that, without genuine effort, true success is unobtainable and unsustainable. This book is not a shortcut to achieving success, and it does not present a foolproof formula for accumulating material rewards and the glowing accolades of your peers. If you are politically connected, or if your dad owns the business in which you will be working, your success is pretty much foreordained, at least in terms of the material rewards you will receive. However, if you are one of the many who want to and will have to actually earn the trappings of success based upon the value of your contributions, this book will point you in the right direction and provide you with the tools you will need to construct a successful career.

The Five Building Blocks of Success are straightforward and easy to understand.

Your Work Ethic

Wanting to succeed does not necessarily lead to success. The desire to succeed must be coupled with performance on the job, and the performance levels have to be high. Hard work, smart work, effort, and consistency are key elements.

Interactions with Others

It is difficult, if not impossible, to be successful if you are not respected, or even liked, by your peers as well as those above your level in the organization. Being able to interact well with people is a basic necessity on the journey towards success.

Teamwork

Either directly or indirectly, you will eventually become a member of a team within your organization. The collective success you help generate will reflect positively on your individual development in the eyes of those above you in the organization.

Creativity—The Search for New Answers

Doing things the same way but expecting different results has been offered as the definition of insanity. When new challenges arise, you will be most successful if you can contribute fresh approaches and innovative solutions.

Thinking Outside of the Box—Using Old Answers in New Ways

Being able to look at challenges and issues from a new perspective often leads to simple solutions for complex problems. You will position yourself as a successful contributor if you continually develop to remain ahead of the curve.

On the front lawn of a community church near my home there is a movie-theater-marquee-type sign. For several weeks it contained this message: *Having a vision without a plan to achieve it is simply a dream*. Though this was offered as food for thought from a religious perspective, I believe that this statement is very appropriate for your quest to achieve success in your business career. Success does not just happen—except for a lucky few. You must take deliberate and focused steps in developing your own action plan if you are to realize the vision of success.

The next to the last point I will make before embarking upon our journey is that the ideas presented in this book are intended to be applied in a business environment. While I believe that my approach to achieving success can and does apply in other environments such as associations, academia, and not-for-profit endeavors, the examples I will use and refer to throughout the text will relate specifically to the for-profit world of commercial business.

The last point I want to cover is the common fallacy about concepts we might regard as "obvious." The old saying that hindsight is 20/20 simply means that many things seem obvious after the fact. It may sound obvious if I tell you that a good work ethic will be instrumental in your search for success. Yet, I have given many performance appraisals and have reviewed many, many more where one of the suggested areas of improvement is work ethic. Just because a point seems "obvious" to some people does not mean that it is obvious to others. So do not assume that thinking about and acting on statements of the "obvious" will not bear fruit. Being reminded beforehand of the "obvious" is quite a bit better than being reprimanded afterwards because you overlooked it.

The Five Building Blocks of Success

Your Work Ethic
It All Starts with YOU

In order to succeed in anything, you need a number of important things:

- The proper education, ability, or skill set
- The proper tools and resources, when and where appropriate
- A clear understanding of the task at hand
- A desire to perform to the best of your ability
- A desire to continually improve yourself

Before I begin to delve further into this list, let us first talk about the phrase **work ethic** in general terms.

People work for a variety of reasons, including economic need and the desire to fill available time with a meaningful endeavor. If not for economic need, a hobby would do nicely to fill in the open hours of the day. So, people work because they have the time and need the money. These appear to be the most basic reasons, with economic need being the primary reason.

We will use the phrase "**work ethic**" to describe a person's desire, or lack thereof, to fulfill the requirements and responsibilities of his or her position at performance levels that range from totally acceptable to totally unacceptable. Thus, your work ethic may be good, or it may be poor. Understanding where you stand as an individual on this scale will permit you to gauge your performance against that of others and to establish a benchmark against which you can measure your future development. In simple terms, understanding your position on the scale will enable you and others—for example, your boss—to determine if you have a good work ethic or a bad work ethic.

Everyone is not destined to be a superstar, achieving high levels of success. Nor is everyone predetermined to simply be average in his or her performance level. Most people do have the ability to improve their performance if they choose to do so.

Some people work hard at working hard. They arrive at their desk or workstation early and stay late. They take great pride in putting in the hours and are referred to by other as workaholics. Those who not only habitually arrive late but also seem to excel in finding an endless supply of excuses for having to leave early, or at least not work as hard as their peers, balance out these hard working people. And in the middle of this broad spectrum we have the majority of people who simply do a good job of trying to do a good job. These people take pride in their work.

Working hard and working smart are two very different things. Long hours and a sweat-covered brow do not necessarily guarantee that the result of those efforts will be considered good work. Some people have to work hard just to be mediocre in their performance, while others seem to coast along easily while accomplishing a great deal. Working smart is working with a focused and dedicated effort and using appropriate abilities and skill sets to maximize the results of the efforts expended.

With the last several paragraphs as a backdrop, let us explore the issues involved in your work ethic in more detail.

The Proper Education, Ability, and/or Skill Set

It stands to reason that, in order to be successful, one needs the education and training to do the job in the first place. You cannot simply rely on a desire to ensure success. You cannot be a doctor simply because you want to be one—clearly, you need a medical degree and some time-in-grade in a medical facility before you can hang out your shingle and announce to the world that you are, in fact, a practicing doctor.

The world of business does not limit itself to employing only college graduates. Nor does it employ only those with master's degrees. In fact, the business community is populated with individuals who have a broad range of educational backgrounds including:

- High school degrees (and partial completion)
- Associate degrees
- Trade school certificates
- College degrees (and partial completion)
- Master's degrees
- PhDs
- Abilities and skill sets that are self taught
- Abilities and skill sets learned at "the school of hard knocks"

Each and every job has its own minimum educational requirements that obviously vary in direct proportion to the degree of complexity of the responsibilities of the position. If you are applying for an entry-level position in the mailroom, you will probably be required to have at least a high school diploma. Apply for an entry-level job at the world's premier investment banking institution, and you will probably need a master's degree from a prestigious East Coast university. Further, some companies—especially for some entry-level positions—arbitrarily require some educational accomplishments beyond those actually required for a position. This is done to ensure that employees can be promoted to the next level, which may require more education.

Remember, I am making these statements with an underlying assumption that you are not currently working within a given organization. Before you are hired, your educational background is your pedigree. After you are hired, while education remains important, it becomes just one of several measurements for use by your management in determining raises and promotions. Actual performance levels and potential are two other aspects that will be taken into account in determining your eventual future within the organization.

In large organizations—even in many small and mid-sized enterprises—there are historical precedents set by individuals who have become successful even though they did not have what we would now refer to as the minimum educational requirements to fulfill any specific position. In the old days, it was conceivable that a person could start in that mailroom job with just a high school diploma and by the end of his or her career, retire as the president or some other executive-level position based upon performance. In today's corporate environment, it would be rare indeed to find this type of bottom-to-top career path repeated and, even if it were, it would most likely apply only to one or two individuals out of a universe of hundreds of thousands of employees.

Once hired, you are typically exposed to additional opportunities to increase your knowledge and skills:

- On-the-job training
- Seminars and courses taught by in-house human resources and/or training department representatives
- Subject-specific seminars and courses taught by equipment suppliers that teach workers skills like how to use a piece of equipment or computer software
- Generic seminars taught by outside resources on such skills as negotiations and communications skills
- Additional college-level courses taught at junior or four-year colleges that provide new skills or keep an existing skill set up to date
- Individual reading and research—either hard copy or Internet

Of all the skill sets that are important in any job, here are three that are truly important:

- Computer skills
- Communication skills, oral and written
- Sales skills

Almost every business relies heavily on computers, either as a main element of the business they are engaged in (e.g., Microsoft, Intel, Dell) or in support of whatever goods or services they are providing to the community (e.g., internal accounting system, HR database). Being able to use a computer and some of the more common software programs (e.g., word processing, spreadsheets, database configuration, presentations) will go a long way in helping you contribute to the overall success of any enterprise regardless of what your initial assignment may be. Further, having the skill to navigate the Internet will open up other valuable sources of information as the need arises.

Oral and written communication skills are basic skills that are used by virtually everyone day in and day out. Being able to clearly and concisely communicate your ideas is of paramount importance. Much time (and, therefore, money) is wasted when issues have to be addressed a second time because they were not communicated clearly the first time.

Sales skills are the most often overlooked skill set element, especially by those who do not have any direct sales responsibilities. People feel that, since they work in human resources, manufacturing, or the accounting department, sales skills are unnecessary. This couldn't be further from the truth. We are all selling, all of the time. We are selling our ideas to others. We are trying to persuade people to understand and accept our points of view. The problem is that most people do not recognize these instances as sales opportunities. If they did, and had honed a basic set of sales skills, they would have a significantly easier time in trying to get others to agree with their requests or point of view.

The Proper Tools and Resources, When and Where Appropriate

Your educational background, as well as any additional training you receive during your career, will be the starting point for your journey toward success. To assist you, you will need, and most likely be given, the tools you will need along the way as well as access to other resources that will assist you in the performance of your duties and responsibilities. A good manager or supervisor will ensure that employees have on hand what is necessary to be successful.

There are times when the proper tools and access to useful resources are handed out like candy at Halloween: Here you go, and would you like some more? There are other times when the simplest requests, such as the need for updated computer software, seem to fall on deaf ears. Each organization has its own guidelines and standards regarding the availability of tools and resources. Remember, businesses exist to make a profit and, while an argument can be made that giving its employees the proper tools and providing access to useful resources will improve profitability, many businesses, managed on a quarter-to-quarter basis, may see these investments as unnecessary expenses.

When the proper tools and access to useful resources are available, make sure you actively seek them out and put them to good use. When they are not available, you may need to factor this lack of resources into your growth and development plans. You might be able to achieve success via alternative routes, or you may find yourself having to face the fact that you, unfortunately, are not working for a company that values its employees.

A Clear Understanding of the Task at Hand

One cannot complete a journey without knowing the final destination. Randomly wandering in search of something—anything—does not make for a very pleasant journey, especially when it's your career journey. And while there is a great deal to be said about the adventures associated with spontaneity, in the working environment you should have a crystal clear understanding of what is expected of you. You should be aware of your responsibilities, the level of authority you have to accomplish those responsibilities, and the accountability that accrues to your performance record in accomplishing those responsibilities.

Many organizations provide job or position descriptions for all positions that document what each employee is responsible for. Sometimes the responsibilities are described in elaborate detail, and sometimes the responsibilities are rather broadly described. While it is the responsibility of management to make sure that each employee is aware of his or her responsibilities and duties, smart employees make sure they also know what is expected of them.

Another layer in your job or position description involves not only the expectations of the enterprise—the literal words included in the document—but also the expectations of your immediate supervisor, who may have a slightly different slant as to how and when specific duties should be performed. In order to be truly successful, there must be alignment between your understanding of your duties and responsibilities and the understanding your immediate supervisor has of them.

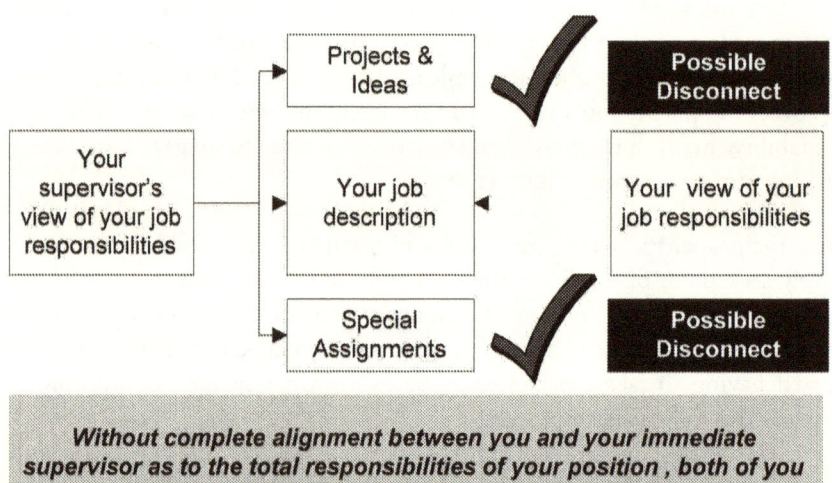

Without complete alignment between you and your immediate supervisor as to the total responsibilities of your position , both of you will be disappointed in the end product of your efforts.

As you rise up the corporate ladder, it is quite possible you could be promoted into a position for which no position description is available. And your immediate supervisor may not always tell you in great detail what he or she expects of you. You will find yourself in a "sink or swim" situation. If you have prepared yourself for upward mobility, you will find ways to adapt and overcome this seeming—or actual—lack of direction. If you are unprepared, or have been promoted beyond your skill set, you may ultimately fail unless you take immediate and deliberate steps to develop the skills necessary for a new, higher-level position.

A Desire to Perform to the Best of Your Ability

There are thoroughbreds and plow horses. There are hunters and gatherers. There are bosses and subordinates. There are stars and problem children.

A lot of analogies and cute titles have been used to describe the various levels of performance. Are all great performers successful? No. Some people feel successful if they do the best they can each and every day. They may not want the headaches of being promoted. They may not want the additional hours away from home required by many mid- and senior-level management positions. They simply are content to do a great job fulfilling their current responsibilities to the best of their abilities.

It is important to make this point here because some people really view success through the rose-colored glasses of material possessions. If you are not the boss, do not have a Rolex, do not drive a mint-condition '87 Buick Grand National, and do not have a summer home in western Michigan, how can you call yourself a success? Some people spend more time engaging in office politics, ensuring the next raise and/or promotion, or negotiating a better option package than they do improving the profitability of the enterprise. Why? They believe that they have achieved success because of the position he or she occupies on the organization chart. And in the material sense, it is hard to argue that they are not success-ful. However, when push comes to shove and you ask these people to actually contribute something meaningful to the organization, they quickly demonstrate their inability to do so. Many times when people finally get the corner office with the big windows their work ethic goes into deep hibernation. After all, there are people below them who actually do the work, right?

A Desire to Continuously Improve Oneself

The only constant in today's global business environment is the ever-increasing rate of change. Changes in technologies, customer expectations, political climates, and the economy occur at an increasing pace and, unless you continue to grow and develop along with these changes, you will quickly be left behind.

An old saying suggests that what got you to where you are will not keep you there. Thus, continuous improvement is the watchword phrase of this rapidly changing world in which we live.

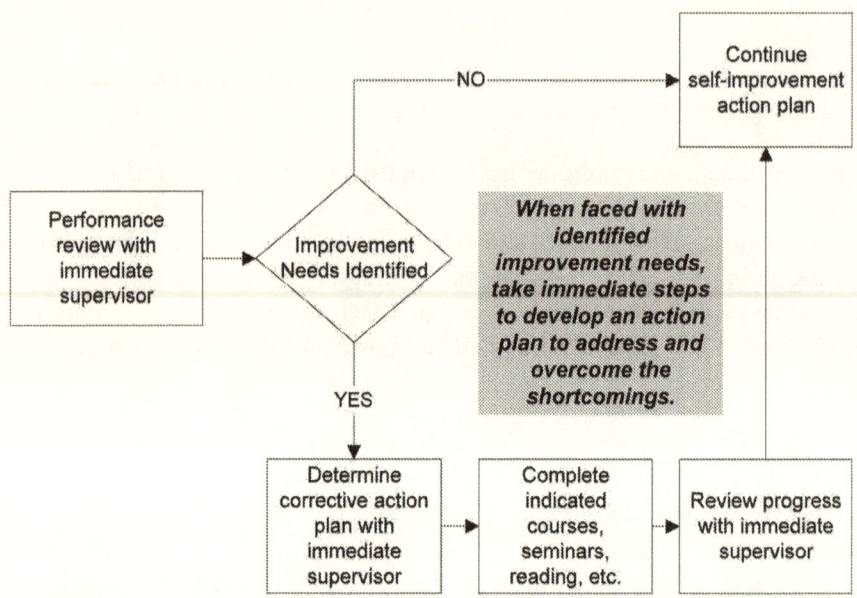

It is very easy to get lulled into a false sense of security regarding any position you hold. Your skill set may meet the requirements of the position and your performance may be acceptable. Yet, as the organization in which you work continues to evolve in reaction to changes in the global business community, it, too, will eventually have to change, or lose touch with its competitors and eventually fail. And even if the pressure is not global and only comes from local, domestic competitors, externally generated changes will require a corresponding response from your organization.

To be truly successful you must proactively seek out information regarding the many changes that are taking place around you and determine which, if any, will have an impact on your career. Sometimes the impact is obvious and immediate. At other times, the impact may be less apparent and may not strike until some time in the future. Preparing yourself to tackle and overcome the challenges brought on by these changes is a positive, proactive course to follow.

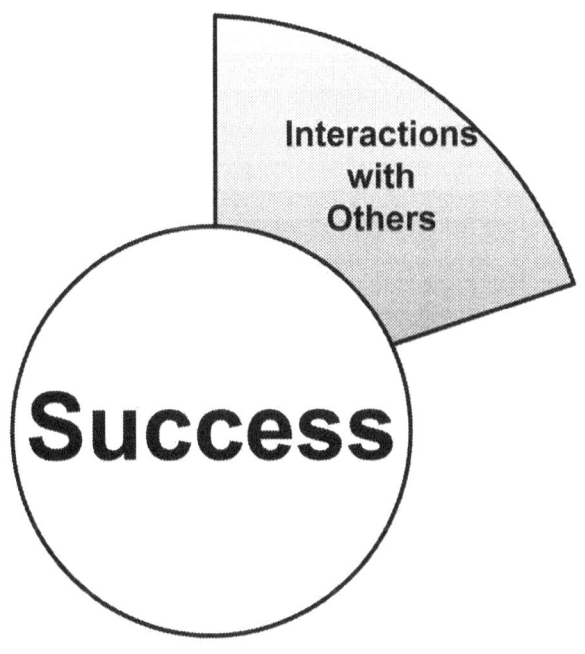

Interactions with Others
Treat Others as You Wish to be Treated

First of all, I am in no position to preach to you about what is or is not acceptable behavior. Only you can determine what type of person you want to be—will be—and, correspondingly, how you will treat others.

Second, I do firmly believe in the subtitle of this section: Treat Others as You Wish to be Treated.

We all hear about companies that have reputations for being nice places to work, where employees are treated with respect. We also hear horror stories of how other companies really are terrible places to work, where the employees are treated as assets to be used and ultimately discarded. What makes a good place to work good, and what makes a bad place to work bad? After all, a basic assumption is that the enterprise exists to make profits for the owners, so why the difference in approaches? Doesn't a history of end results suggest that one approach is truly better than the other? Let's start with the basic premise—the one about the enterprise existing to generate profits for the owners.

Profits for the Owners

Ask owners why they own a company, or own stock in a company, and the answer will be that they hope to make money. I imagine somewhere there is some fifth-generation owner of a small business who keeps Bob's Buggy Whips Unlimited open as a tribute to dear old great-, great-, great-grandpa, but, by and large, the vast majority of owners own for the purpose of making money. Except for companies owned and operated by only one individual, a company has at least two employees. Frank owns the lawn maintenance company and Joe is the guy that maintains the lawns.

In this example of a small company—one owner and one employee in the lawn maintenance business—it would be nice if the owner treated the employee nicely, but this is not a business requirement. The margins in lawn maintenance are probably pretty slim and, since the skill set necessary to cut the grass, trim the lawn, and rake up the leaves is not very demanding, any number of individuals can perform the work. Even with the low wages and lack of fringe benefits offered by many lawn-care businesses there is a rather large pool of available workers. So, to a degree, one can make the argument that labor supply and demand has an influence on how the owner may see how he must treat his employees. However, if we attempt to use this logic to justify our actions towards others, we are sacrificing free will. "I don't have to treat him nicely, because others will do the job if he doesn't like the way he is being treated" is a very shallow argument, at least in my humble opinion. In fact, being nice when the circumstances don't require it—as if we need justification to be nice in the first place—is what being nice is all about.

Being nice does not mean that the owner of our lawn maintenance business needs to over compensate his employee. It does not mean he has to offer anything over and above what his competitors are doing for their employees in terms of perks and/or benefits. It would be nice if he did, but he doesn't have to. Yet, he still can be nice to his employee. And he can be nice *and* also have high expectations of his employee's performance on the job. In other words, you can be fair, yet firm in your management style. You can have high expectations for an employee's performance level, but you must also ensure that employees have the proper training and proper tools in order to accomplish their assignments. You can treat people with dignity and respect without sacrificing your overall goal of obtaining and maintaining a profit margin.

You must also remember that a relationship, whether casual or formal, is a two-way street. In our lawn maintenance scenario, the employee should also treat his boss with dignity and respect.

Before I started my consulting business—my friends tease me by saying "when you had a real job"—I came into contact with a company that used "Fair, Firm, Friendly" as a slogan for the relationships that were expected to be maintained by all of its employees. This included relationships with one's peer group, those under and those above on the organization chart, and customers as well as suppliers. I'm not sure if this approach was home grown within that particular organization, or if it came courtesy of another consultant. I heard the phrase only one or two times, and never really saw it in practice, at least in the relationships the individuals in our company had with the individuals in that company. My company was trying—successfully, I might add—to sell services to that company. I witnessed the friendliness of the relationships between our contacts and theirs, I really saw the firmness of their convictions, wants and desires, but I really never saw the fairness in their approach. After all, they were the customer and the customer is always right.

Yet, whether or not the Fair, Firm, Friendly mantra was a well-thought-out, long-term philosophy or a flavor-of-the-month idea of some executive, the approach, I believe, has some merit for further discussion in terms of how you should consider treating others.

My Interpretation of Fair, Firm, Friendly

- Fairness
    - o The fact that certain beliefs and convictions are held by one group does not automatically make them right—or even appropriate—for other groups.
    - o Each of us has a personal interpretation of right and wrong.
    - o We can uncover and understand helpful information if we listen to people's positions and the reasons for their beliefs—even if their ideas are contrary to our own.
    - o When appropriate, compromise is not a bad word.

- Firmness
    - o Recognize the reasons that you believe what you believe, and be able to articulate these reasons calmly and concisely when dealing with others.
    - o If a belief cannot be supported by some basis in fact, it is simply an opinion, which, given the introduction of new information, is subject to change.
    - o Recognize the limits of authority when negotiating the position established by others (e.g., someone in a procurement capacity for a company must follow and support the direction established by the "users" and "decision makers" with regard to the goods or services that are being purchased).

- Friendliness
    - o Being friendly in our interactions with others does not automatically generate the need for compromising our fairness or firmness.
    - o Establishing a good rapport with our co-workers is instrumental in maximizing everyone's contribution to the overall good of the organization.
    - o A friendly working environment does not demand a total alignment or realignment of beliefs on the part of the individuals involved in the relationships.

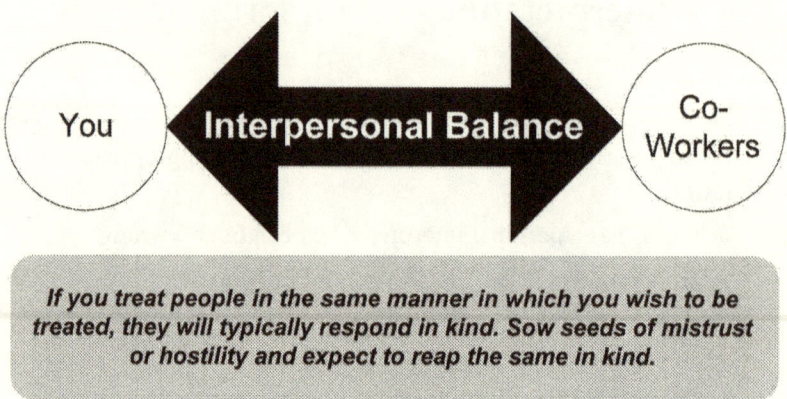

If you treat people in the same manner in which you wish to be treated, they will typically respond in kind. Sow seeds of mistrust or hostility and expect to reap the same in kind.

So, if you are friendly in your dealings with others, are fair in the give-and-take aspects of your interactions, and firm in the convictions and/or responsibilities that are not open for compromise, you will most likely be operating in a productive and positive working environment.

Negative Role Models

Clearly, people change and society evolves. Many years ago it was acceptable to issue corporal punishment to an unruly student. In today's politically correct environment, even yelling at an unruly student is, in most cases, forbidden. Of course, this street runs both ways. In the old days, if a teacher caught you with a small pocketknife in your backpack, chances were that he or she would smack you across the wrist and take the knife away. Nowadays, if you're caught with a nail clipper, you face expulsion.

Let us look at people who grow up—in the business sense—under "bad" bosses. Bad bosses can so negatively influence subordinates, that when the subordinates eventually become bosses themselves, they are in danger of viewing their new position as an opportunity for "payback." Their new subordinates will now get the opportunity to feel what it is like to have a real jerk for a boss. This vicious cycle really is uncalled for and it is detrimental to everyone involved. Obviously, this does not happen every time, but, based upon my experiences, approximately 30 percent of the people who are promoted into a supervisory role are either subsequently demoted or find themselves stuck in that role because of their poor people skills.

So, what's the message here? What does this example demonstrate?

The basic message is that people are the products of their environment, and good as well as bad can influence people in their outlook and treatment of others. Your interactions with your co-workers can be productive, positive, and mutually beneficial, or they can be counterproductive, negative, and beneficial to no one.

Bad bosses will provide you with plenty of examples of how to treat people poorly. Do your best to avoid using them as a role model in your developmental efforts.

Sometimes it is easy to pick up some bad interpersonal skills from others, especially people in authority. If your boss is successful, though he does quite a bit of yelling, you might think that, in order to be productive, you'll have to yell, too, when you become boss.

Some people are just challenged when it comes to their social skills with others. Their home life might have been strained and, unfortunately, constant battling on the home front can make people defensive, full of suspicion of others, and possessing interpersonal skills that clearly need some polishing.

Positive Role Models

People tend to work best when they deal with people they like and with people who like them in return. Share a warm smile and a friendly "hello" with co-workers in the morning and they will typically respond in kind. Be considerate of other people and offer to help when you think you may be able to lend assistance on a problem or an assignment. Later, when you need help, people will come to your aid as well. Sometimes, just knowing that someone is willing to offer some friendly assistance enables people to look beyond any problems at hand and realize that they have a friend who cares.

Now I am not suggesting we all become Caspar Milquetoast. You do not have to go belly up to everyone, as a sign of submission, like the runt in the litter. But, in the long run, it is a lot more enjoyable to participate in a positive working environment than in a negative one.

Some suggestions to consider when working with others include:

- The basic rule is: treat others as you wish to be treated.
- Really listen—don't spend your listening time planning your response.
- Respect the opinions and beliefs of others, especially when their cultural or ethnic backgrounds differ from your own
- Make sure your body language is not sending a message that is contradictory to your spoken message.
- Some people's beliefs and ideas may be different from yours simply because you are in possession of different sets of information.
- Successful relationships are built when both partners are able to give and take.

People who treat each other with respect and dignity will tend to work together effectively, creating an environment that is both pleasant and productive.

All in all, you are responsible for the way you interact with people. Treat them nicely, with cooperation and help, and, in most cases, you will receive the same in return. Treat people poorly and you will reap what you have sown, and in times of real need, you will be disappointed and sad that no one came to your assistance.

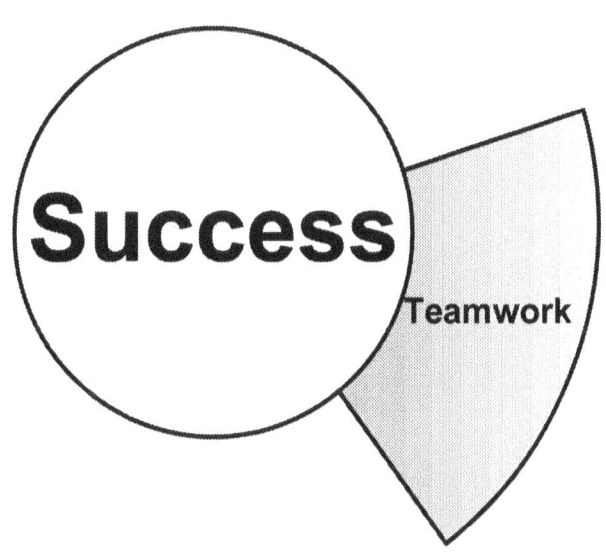

Teamwork
Positive Collective Efforts Benefit
Everyone

Sooner or later almost everyone becomes part of either a formal or informal team. Even as the owner and sole employee of my one-person consulting company, I have an informal team. My lawyer and my tax accountant assist and guide me as we navigate the myriad of details in both the state and federal tax codes. Then I have a group of friends who form an informal network. I know these people because, when I worked as an employee (my "real" job), I used to work with them, or I used to sell to them. These people help me with leads and contact information. I also have developed a new network comprised of suppliers who used to sell to the companies I worked for and some new contacts I have made while selling the services of my consulting company. And finally, my last team is a small group of friends who have been kind enough to act as advisors to me and offer constructive criticism from time to time that helps keep my business on track.

When a client engages my company, I form a team with some designated representatives of the client in addressing the issue or solving the problem they have identified. At other times, the engagement may be for the purpose of developing a strategy to take advantage of an opportunity the client has uncovered. These assignments require a team approach as well.

Let us define the concept of *team* before we proceed any further. THE NEW INTERNATIONAL WEBSTER'S POCKET DICTIONARY OF THE ENGLISH LANGUAGE, published by Trident Press International (1997), defines team as:

> *A group of people working or playing together as a unit, esp. a group forming one side of a contest.*

It is interesting to note that this is the second definition of the noun "team" in the dictionary. The first one is, "Two or more beasts of burden harnessed together." Unfortunately, many companies and many managers do look upon their workers as beasts of burden if one is to judge by the way they are treated. But, that is fodder for another book. Let's concentrate on the positive definition, definition #2: *a group of people working or playing together as a unit.*

Teamwork is a Two-Layered Concept

The first layer of the concept of teamwork is the implied necessity that individual team members must strive to perform to the best of their own abilities. I stress "implied necessity" because it is a fundamental belief of mine that individuals who are successful must strive to be successful. Success, more often than not, is a direct result of hard work and outstanding performance. Each of us has our own work ethic, which we have already discussed in this book. Those of us who desire to be successful realize that a positive and concerted effort must be expended in both becoming and remaining successful in any particular endeavor.

As a side bar, I will acknowledge that some people achieve the trappings of success without having to truly achieve what we refer to herein as performance-based success. These individuals are born into it, or marry into it, or win the lottery, or one day simply wake up having access to riches and power. It is up to them as individuals to back up that visible manifestation of success with their performance. Either they will, or they will not.

It is interesting to note that a number of people who have been given the many trappings of success through their families, luck at the lottery, and so forth, really believe that they are truly successful simply because they have access to the material trappings of success. I will acknowledge publicly that I am envious of their material trappings. However, I believe that they cannot lay claim to having earned the trappings on the basis of their performance, and they should not represent to others that their performance warrants such rewards unless the underlying performance is truly there in the first place.

The second layer of the team concept is the recognition that the probability for the success of the team is dramatically enhanced in direct proportion to the team's ability to focus the collective best efforts of each of the team members. Simply put, this is the old saying that 1 + 1 can be greater than 2.

So, we have team members who are working to achieve their personal best as individuals. Also, through interaction with other team members, each is able to maximize his or her individual contribution when it is combined into a collective effort that satisfies the goal of the team.

Why Teams are Created

Teams are established for one of several specific purposes:
- To win—or retain—something of value
  - o To become a key supplier to a major consumer of the products and/or services produced by the enterprise
  - o To obtain an increase in market share
  - o To remain a supplier to a major current customer
- To discover a solution to a problem
  - o To find a cure for cancer
  - o To resolve the software glitch in the new release
  - o To use a new logistics program to speed up deliveries
- To achieve a previously unattained level of performance
  - o To attain a zero defects level of quality in manufacturing
  - o To develop software that downloads digital information twice as fast as our largest competitor's software

While there are probably many more categories we could conjure up as to why teams are created, these three descriptions will serve us well as we continue to develop this topic further.

The duration of the life of a team varies depending on the reason for its initial creation. Some teams, such as research and development teams, may exist for extended periods of time as companies continue in their quest to bring new products to the market. Even though the length of time served by any individual team member may vary, the team—as a whole—continues to exist so long as the need for the team exists. In other cases, a team may exist for a relatively brief period. The goal of a short-term team may be to develop the theme for the next marketing campaign. Once the theme has been identified, refined, and agreed to, the team disbands.

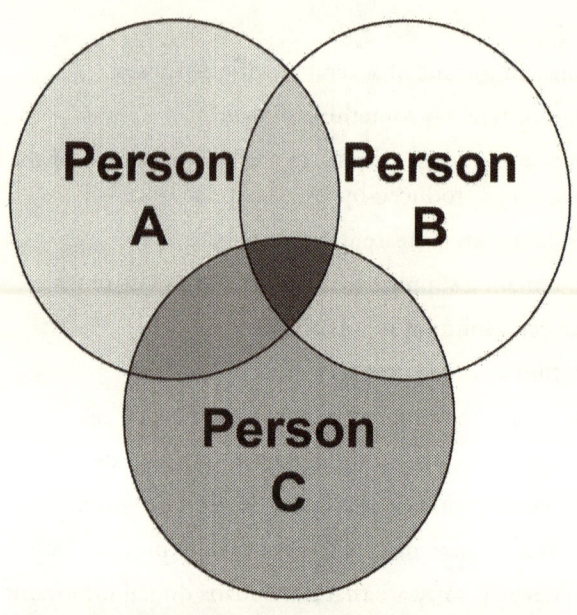

The collective efforts of all of the members on a team surpass the value of the efforts when measured separately.

The Contest

If you will recall, the definition of team that I quoted from *Webster* a couple of pages earlier also included the phrase "a group forming one side of a contest." There is always a real—or at least a perceived—benefit in accomplishing whatever goals have been set for a team—the purpose for establishing the team in the first place.

In the business world, goals tend to be simple in their description:

- Take the ABC account away from our largest competitor
- Prevent our largest competitor from taking the XYZ account away from us

- Find a way to reduce waste by 25%
- Find a way to increase profits by 15%
- Find a way to reduce overhead expenses by 5%

It is obvious in some cases what the contest is all about and who the contestants are. In our example—take the ABC account away from our largest competitor—the contest is between our firm and our largest competitor. The prize is the ABC account. Both of our firms are interested in having representatives from the ABC account sign a contract to purchase the goods and/or services we offer. The process may be very structured, with formal requests for information, supplier visits, tours of manufacturing facilities, requests for proposals, and requests for last and final offers occurring at the appropriate times. Or, the process may be less formal and consist simply of meetings, proposals, and negotiations. Both sides present their proposals and, usually, after a negotiations process, the ABC representatives either sign a contract with us and we win, or they remain with our competitor and we lose. After the sales process has run its course and a final decision has been announced, the winner typically celebrates while the loser rushes to perform an autopsy to determine why they lost.

People—companies—buy from people they like. This is an old sales adage. This reality is the reason that salespeople try to establish a positive rapport with customers and potential customers. The rationale behind this sales strategy is this: if the potential customer likes me, he will let me know that my price is too high, or my delivery schedule is too long, and give me an opportunity to revise my offer, as opposed to simply saying "no thanks" and going to a competitor of mine.

Populating the Team

I will use this example—take the ABC account away from our largest competitor—to discuss the selection process for populating a team that is being established to accomplish a specific task. In this case, the task is to develop a sales strategy targeted at capturing an important account that is currently under contract with a major competitor of ours. You will need the assistance of the following types of individuals:

- A strong facilitator who can not only keep the group focused on the mission at hand, but can also contribute a fair share of ideas, and actually help to accomplish some of the myriad of tasks that will eventually result in the finished product of the group effort

- The sales representative(s)—and manager, sales VP, or even sales senior VP—who are charged with handling the opportunity and making the sale

- Some people familiar with the sales process to help identify the basic sales strategy as well as the sales tactics that will be used by the sales people assigned to handle the sales process with representatives of the prospective account

- Someone with personal knowledge of the target account as a company as well as anyone with personal knowledge about the representatives from that company who will be involved in the sales/buying process

- Someone who can contribute analytical skills to assist in the determination of pricing points and profitability issues

- Creative people who can assist in the development of presentation material, collateral materials, and the actual proposal

- Someone with knowledge of the suppliers that must be relied on to produce the goods and/or services we are trying to sell

- Someone who can provide legal counsel and assist in the development of the contractual language that will be provided along with our final proposal

- Clerical assistance to help in the generation of reports, analyses, presentations, and samples

Clearly, this list is only meant to be representative. It seems appropriate if the team is to achieve its goal of "getting" the ABC account. There are many types of real life applications for teams; the goals dictate the specific types of individuals who should be involved.

Populating a team with dedicated, intelligent and capable individuals will dramatically increase its productivity, especially if the team leader is an accomplished facilitator.

Care should be taken to make sure each individual selected to participate on a team has:

- A willingness to participate
- A desire to succeed
- A skill set that matches the requirements
- The ability to work well with others
- The ability to communicate effectively
- Availability

Some of the team members will be required to participate in every meeting. Others may need to participate only when areas that pertain to their special expertise are on the agenda. In our example, legal representative may be needed when the contractual language of the proposal is discussed. If a draft contract that protects our interests as well as those of the potential customer is required, the legal representative may be able to work alone for an extended period of time, only rejoining the group when his portion of the work is ready for review.

The frequency with which the team meets will vary from assignment to assignment. Meetings for the sake of conducting a meeting are most unproductive, and establishing a meeting schedule that is too burdensome will truly detract from the team members' enthusiasm.

An initial meeting might consist of the following:

- Explanation of why the team has been formed
- Brief outline of each team member's specific area of expertise
- Presentation of the timeline dictated by the opportunity—in days, weeks, months, years
- Proposal of the frequency of future meetings
- Identification of specific discipline-related tasks
- Blue-sky discussions—explored in greater detail in another section of this book—to identify new approaches and ideas
- The reporting structure of the team
- The reporting method(s) of the team—hard copy reports vs. digital, presentation formats, economic models, review and approval process protocols, et cetera

Follow-up meetings might cover:

- Status report from each discipline
- Introduction and review of new facts
- Time line adjustments, if any
- Review and discussion of previously submitted draft reports
- Assignment of new tasks

Meetings will typically continue until the final collective effort is completed. In our example, the final effort would include the proposed sales strategy, the final proposal document for submission to the potential customer, any collateral material that is to be submitted along with the proposal, any PowerPoint and/or other presentation material, and samples.

Team Interactions

For the team to function at its best, the following conditions must be satisfied:

- Everyone must understand the overall goal
- Everyone must understand his or her individual role and be able to fulfill it
- The team must be populated with highly motivated individuals
- The team must have access to any required resources
- The team must have an effective leader

Though success is never guaranteed, these resources give any team the highest possibility for success. In our example, despite the best efforts of the team, it is possible that our competition could put forth an even more attractive offer for the ABC account. But it should be clear that a dysfunctional team stands very little chance of being successful and that, in those few instances when a dysfunctional team is successful, pure unadulterated luck is most likely to be the overriding factor.

A dysfunctional team will accomplish little and disappoint many.

Creativity
The Search for New Answers

Creativity—the process of generating a new idea—cannot be taught. Some people are creative, while others are not. But creativity is one of the building blocks of success and, fortunately, exposure to the subject early on in one's career provides ample time to expand our horizons and get comfortable with the idea of how to generate ideas.

Blue-Sky Sessions

Blue-sky discussion sessions bring creativity into a useful arena by encouraging give and take and the free-flowing generation of ideas. Companies—or, most often groups within the company—attempt to try and solve a particular problem, or to take advantage of an apparent opportunity, through blue-sky discussions. To be most effective, the blue-sky session is typically led by a meeting facilitator whose role is to lead the discussion rather than actively participate. The following model is often used as a skeleton around which a blue-sky session can be developed:

- Participants
  - o A solid performer is best suited for the role of facilitator. This individual should have the respect of the other meeting participants and possess previously demonstrated leadership skills. Sometimes, an organization will engage an outside consultant to fulfill the role of facilitator since the responsibility is to facilitate, not to participate. In this regard, an intimate knowledge of the subject to be discussed, the possible solutions, or an intimate knowledge of the personalities of the people who comprise the blue-sky discussion panel is not required.
  - o The rest of the individuals in a blue-sky session will vary depending on the topic, but might include:
    - People with intimate knowledge of the topic to be discussed.
    - People who have previously demonstrated a knack for creativity.
    - People from the area of the company most affected by the topic. For example, if the group's mission is to develop a product that can effectively compete against a competitor's new release, someone from manufacturing, where our new product would be produced, should be in attendance.
    - People who have been identified as high potential individuals. The blue-sky experience will expose them to a broader spectrum

of company representatives, place them in a highly competitive environment, and help them to develop their own creative juices.

- Several subject matter experts who are capable of taking a new idea and developing it.

- Topic
  - o The issue—problem, challenge, opportunity—should be specific in nature and should be presented concisely. The presentation of the topic should not be made as a lead-in to a specific solution. If the topic is too broad, it will be difficult for the group to tackle the issue. For example, if the opportunity is to develop some new product offerings around the new technology just purchased by the manufacturing division, the group can focus in on a meaningful discussion. On the other hand, if the issue is achieving world peace, the group discussion will be overwhelmingly broad and little, if any, progress will be made.

- Rules of engagement
  - o Everyone participating in the meeting should understand and adhere to some basic guidelines, designed to keep the discussion on target:
    - The facilitator rules the meeting. His or her role is to develop momentum and keep it going. This individual will have the power to allow someone to speak, stop a conversation for clarification, or end a conversation when it wanders off of the topic.
    - Even though we often hear "there is no such thing as a bad idea," some ideas *are* just plain bad, and discussing them should not divert the efforts of the group by engaging in meaningless conversations.
    - In spite of the preceding bullet, the following reasons are NOT justification to label an idea as being bad:
      - We tried it before and it didn't work out.
      - We don't do things that way.
      - It wasn't my idea.
      - I don't like the person who thought up the idea.
    - Everyone is entitled to offer opinions and input. It is the role of the facilitator to control the discussion. No one else needs to attempt to control the flow of the discussion.

- Everyone should be respectful of everyone else participating in the blue-sky session. The purpose of the initial meeting is to generate and identify possible solutions—ideas—to resolve the issue at hand. Very little time should be spent attacking an idea and no time should be spent attacking an individual.

- All restrictions should be lifted when considering possible solutions. Funding, head count, technology, market conditions, should all be considered flexible. While this may be unpractical in the short-run (e.g., we do not have access to unlimited funding) being able to consider this funding may act as a catalyst to help generate additional ideas that can be acted upon, developed, and implemented in the short term.

- When all else fails, try redefining the problem and start the process all over again. For example, if we cannot identify any products we could produce to compete effectively against a competitor's new release, we could redefine the problem by asking ourselves what the final consumers are really interested in buying. Chasing a competitor is not always an effective way to compete. Getting a leg up on the competitor by correctly anticipating changing consumer wants and needs is a very effective way to compete.

- One individual, designated as scribe, should be responsible for capturing all ideas on paper. Towards the end of the meeting, when ideas seem to be drying up, the group can work together to rank order these ideas for follow-up action.

- Resources
  - The availability of the people selected to participant.
  - A meeting room equipped with flipcharts, overhead projector, computer, pads and pencils, and, most importantly, an excellent facilitator.

- Meeting length
  - The initial meeting will range from two hours to a full eight-hour day—any shorter and you may curtail creativity; any longer and you will find that people just get too tired and want to go home. The average session should probably last from three to five hours.

  - "We are going to stay here until we think of something" is a counterproductive plan. You can always pick up the session the next morning if necessary, though some will argue that this length of break will result in some people being unable to get back into the proper idea-generating mood the next day. On the other hand, others will argue that this respite will give everyone's mind a chance to recover, so that they will return the next day re-energized.

o   Sometimes it might be more effective to introduce the issue and discuss it for a couple of hours, then break and give people or teams of people some time to independently generate ideas. In a subsequent meeting, people can present their thoughts and follow-up discussions can be held.

- Next steps

o   The main purpose of the initial blue-sky session is to generate a list of possible solutions.

o   The next to last order of business is to prioritize the suggestions for further action.

o   The last order of business is to select which ideas are worthy of immediate further consideration. The selected ideas are then presented as a goal for the various constituencies—manufacturing, sales, accounting—to develop strategies and tactics that will enable them to achieve their portion of the overall goal.

o   Future meeting will be held as necessary to review progress, introduce new information, and, eventually, agree upon the final composition of the proposed solution.

Limits to Creativity

There are three levels of knowledge:
1. Things that you know
2. Things that you know you don't know
3. Things you don't know that you don't know

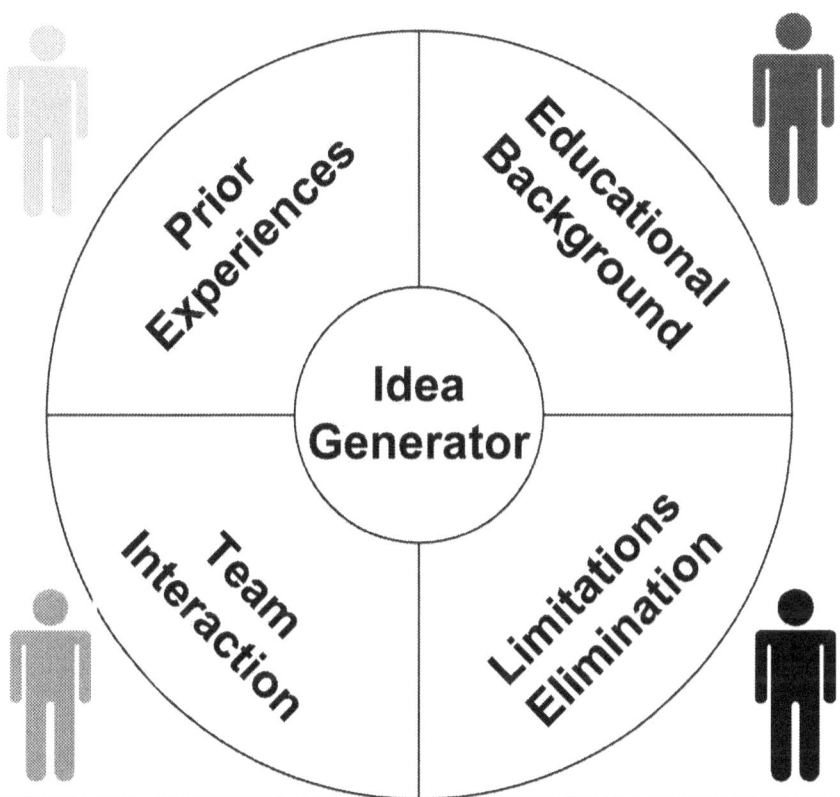

The members of a successful BLUE-SKY team will respond to an initial idea with comments, suggestions and modifications in an on-going effort to create a viable solution. Quite often, a well focused session will generate several alternative ideas that should be prioritized and eventually investigated for possible future implementation.

When we find ourselves faced with the need to be creative, the first level of knowledge we access is #1—Things that you know. We scan our memory banks and pull out whatever information we can find based on our educational background, work experiences, or general life experiences. We also foray out beyond "factual information" and access our own personal wants, needs, and desires in an attempt to be as creative as possible.

The second level of knowledge we access is #2—Things that you know you don't know. As an example, you may not know anything about how to conduct brain surgery, but maybe an operation on the brain would save the patient, so you might suggest this as a possible solution. In the case of the #2 level of knowledge, as we accesses our memory banks, we usually come up either empty handed, or with a handful of disjointed, seemingly meaningless bits of facts or opinions, or something we recall reading in a book. We string these bits and pieces together to form what may or may not be the outline of an idea.

Obviously, the last level of knowledge, #3—Things you don't know you don't know, is, on the surface, an empty pot. If you truly don't know something, you simply don't know it. However, given the right amount of stimulation—additional information—your brain may actually be able to access some deeper level memories that actually can be brought to bear on helping to develop a solution. For example, you may not have had any prior understanding about the theory of cold fusion. During a blue-sky session, someone suggests cold fusion as a possible solution to a given problem. You ask for additional information, which you receive. All of a sudden you remember something similar in concept and offer it up to the group for consideration. In other words, one person's idea is often the springboard to other ideas from other participants. The collective brain can then process this information further, massaging it until an idea springs forth.

Creativity Can Become a Self-Fulfilling Prophecy

Most blue-sky session solutions tend to be the result of the collective effort, with several—or more—individuals contributing to the final idea. Someone says something that causes someone else to add a little bit more. These two fragments cause a third person to articulate the same concept with a slightly different twist. A subject matter expert repeats the idea but adds a practical way of accomplishing it and, before you know it, you have the outline of a workable solution. Whether or not the solution is ultimately practical or economical is something yet to be determined.

The collective effort uses the first two levels of knowledge. The important point to note is that no two people have exactly the same information in their memory banks. Thus, one comment—or idea fragment—can become a catalyst upon which others can build. Ideas and concepts feed off each other and grow until a final idea is achieved.

Often during blue-sky sessions, several ideas emerge as possible solutions. Each has its merits and challenges. Each appears to solve the problem but needs an in-depth analysis to prove out its potential. Once the participants rank order the ideas generated during a blue-sky session, they can develop action plans to determine what next steps are necessary to prove or disprove the practicality and applicability of the proposed solutions.

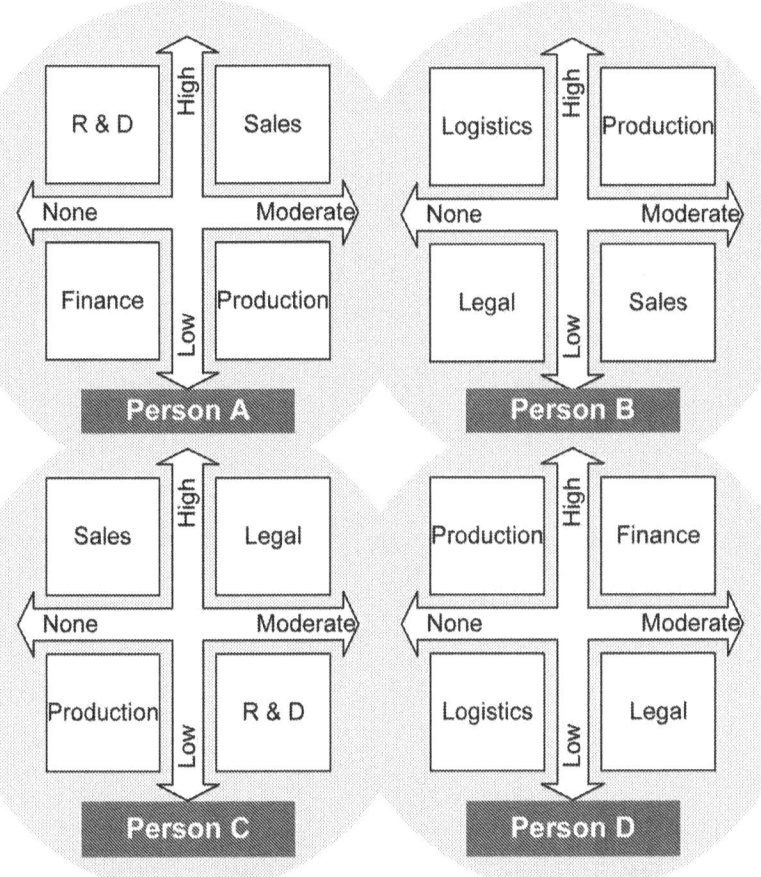

The various participants in a BLUE-SKY session will have varied backgrounds and different levels of knowledge on a variety of topics ranging from a HIGH understanding to NONE. The collective intelligence and experiences of the group will allow each member to act as a catalyst upon which a central idea can be identified, shaped and finalized.

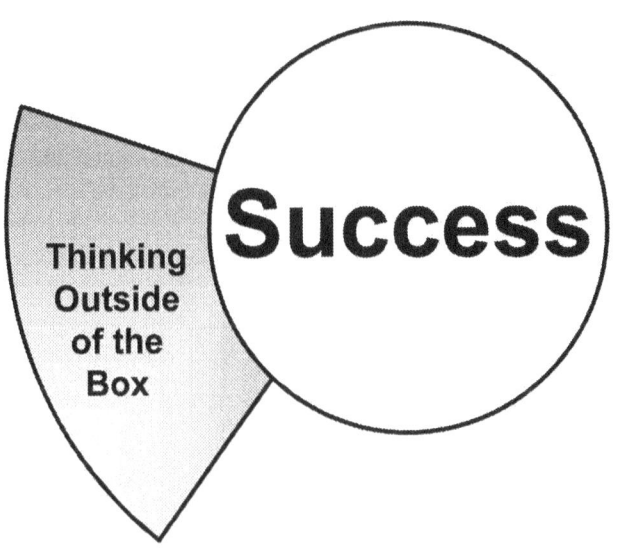

Thinking Outside of the Box
Using Old Answers in New Ways

Many people equate "thinking outside of the box" to creativity. In the previous section we defined creativity as *the process for generating new ideas*. As a differentiator, we will define thinking outside of the box as *using old answers in a new way*. Many of you have encountered the nine-dots exercise. The instruction is to connect all nine dots using only four straight lines *and* not picking up your pencil from the paper once you start.

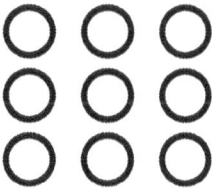

This cannot be accomplished unless one envisions a solution beyond the artificial boundary of the box that the mind's eye perceives when first tackling this challenge. So, the solution, which exists outside of the box, becomes:

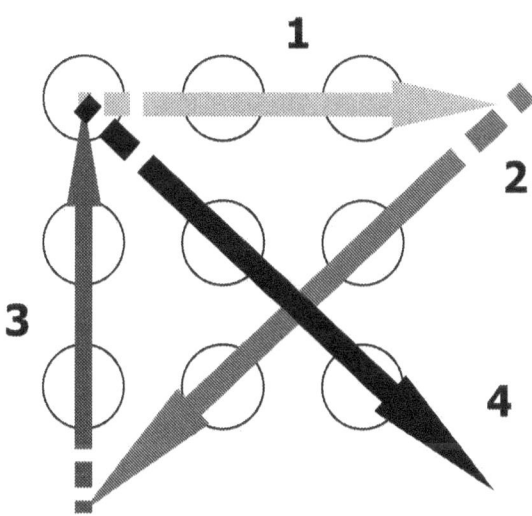

This exercise is important because it drives home the point that people frequently create artificial barriers—seeing the nine dots existing within a box—when faced with a problem. And when we do this, we automatically, and unknowingly, turn a blind eye to what could have been some very simple and obvious solutions.

Outside of the Box Thinking

Individual approaches problem with a fresh perspective and though relying on prior experiences and their educational background, will reach beyond the obvious conclusions in an effort to re-purpose old answers in new ways

Inside the Box Thinking

Individual artificially limits scope of problem solving effort based upon:

**Prior Experiences
Education**

Once the blinders are removed, the individual will be able to see beyond their artificially created barriers.

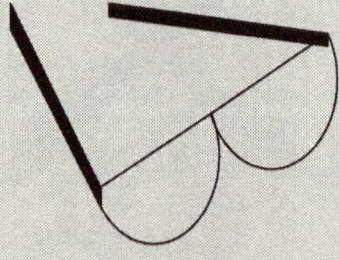

We Create Our Own Limitations

When faced with a problem or a challenge, we are apt to use our personal experiences and educational background as sources for possible solutions. This is understandable. We find comfort in what we know, and most people find confusion and apprehension in the unknown. When faced with a problem or challenge, we look to the past in order to generate possible solutions. The problem with this approach is that, frequently, we focus only on the obvious. Compounding this myopic view and making it even worse, we look at the obvious in obvious ways. And this is much more than a simple semantic difference. An example will really help us to understand this. Here is a real situation I was faced with.

I purchased some chrome wheels for my car. To prevent them from being stolen, I purchased a set of wheel locks, which meant that I had to use a special "key" to remove the locks before I could actually remove the tire and wheel from the car. Over time, the key became worn out and actually ended up breaking while I was in the middle of trying to remove a flat tire, leaving me with a flat tire on a wheel that I couldn't remove from the car. The only good luck was that the car was in the driveway of my house.

For clarification, here is the outline of a typical eight-sided wheel lug nut that can be removed with a standard socket set.

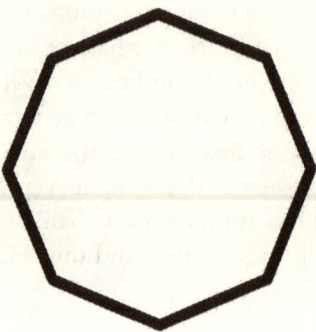

My special, theft-proof locking wheel lug nuts had a smooth exterior and an eight-point-star shape hollowed out of the center where the key fit:

Clearly, a standard socket set would not work. I took one of these wheel locks to several automotive parts stores only to find out that the manufacturer of the wheel locks had long gone out of business and that new keys were simply unavailable. I stopped at the auto repair shop and found that the only solution was to remove the tire by breaking off the lugs. And to do this I would have to have the car towed into the repair shop. Total estimated expenses were over $300 for the towing and the resulting repairs to replace the broken lugs.

Now I wish I could claim that I solved the problem. I did not, but my small contribution was to go to a local tool retailer, explain my problem, and ask if they had any suggestions. The gentleman behind the counter said that he didn't have any keys or anything else that would work, but, as he started to hand the lug nut back to me he said, "Wait a minute." He went out back into the storeroom for a few minutes then returned with a smile on his face. He had solved the problem. He told me that a four-sided 3/8-inch extension bar for a standard socket set fit perfectly into the eight-pointed star opening. He showed me how the four-sided extension fit into the eight-point star snuggly enough to work effectively. When I tried it, just like the man said, it worked like a charm.

This is the profile of the solution:

I, as well as everyone else I had spoken to regarding this challenge, artificially—based only upon our own previous experiences—limited the problem solving effort to trying to identify an eight-point solution. The sales person at the tool retailer redefined the problem from "Where can I find an eight-sided key to solve the problem?" to "What <u>tool</u> will solve the problem?" Within seconds he had arrived at a workable solution. Everyone else saw an eight-point star; he saw two squares at different angles. This is a classic example of how thinking outside of the box, and not imposing limitations on the problem-solving process, really does work.

Order of Magnitude

While one could argue that there are still quite a few similarities between creativity and thinking outside of the box, one other area of differentiation is the factor of significance. Problems, challenges, and opportunities range in size from small to large. Their impact on an organization can be huge or small. Your biggest problem at work may not give anyone else in the organization any concern at all. Suffice it to say, problems, challenges, and opportunities come in all shapes and sizes.

If the potential impact of a problem is significant, the organization will need a creative solution and it is possible that the creative solution will simply be the result of thinking outside of the box by one or more key people. Blue-sky sessions will be held, resources dedicated, and a solution sought. But, if the impact on the organization is small, or it is truly limited to just a department, team, or individual, thinking outside of the box will routinely generate a workable solution.

For example, a production department is faced with the rather typical problem of peaks and valleys in the demand for their products. Sometimes it is 24/7 with everyone on full overtime, while at other times the crew has to stretch things out to just to fill a five-day workweek. These wide swings in demand result in significant extra expenses—like overtime and increased waste—and are disruptive to the crew's personal lives as well.

While it will not work in every production situation, establishing a backlog production scheduling process can help to mitigate these swings, resulting in a more evenly loaded production plan. The outside of the box thinking here is that it may not be necessary to rigidly marry product ordering with production and delivery, as managers might do by limiting their thinking regarding the ordering/production process. If the product allows for it, a company can lessen the peak/valley issue by redistributing the production requirements in a more level manner.

Another example occurs in the sales arena. When a sale is lost, people frequently run around performing an opportunity autopsy to determine why the sale was not made. Sometimes the goal is to find someone to blame for the loss, while at other times there is a genuine interest to learn from past mistakes.

On the other hand, when a company makes the sale, the end result is too often just a celebration. Outside of the box thinking would suggest that an opportunity autopsy should be undertaken on successes as well as failures. Why we did succeed is just as important an issue as why we did not succeed. Did we succeed because our price was too low? Did we offer too many added extras? Or, did the competition withdraw? We really should know if we want to continue being successful in our sales efforts.

Outside of the box thinking does not require special meetings, endless resources, and untold hours of effort. What it does require is the ability to leave preconceived notions behind us as we attempt to look at all problems, challenges, and opportunities with a fresh approach. Of course, not all problems, challenges, and opportunities require outside of the box thinking. Don't go in search of new applications for old solutions if the need does not truly exist.

Every once in a while you will come across what are referred to as "brainteasers." These puzzles, questions, math sequences, and other thought provokers, are designed to test both your knowledge and your ability to reason out a solution. One of my favorites is the question, "How far can a dog run into the woods?" The obvious answer—to some at least—is half way. Then it starts to run out of the woods. Unfortunately many people cloud this simplistic query with demands for additional information, which may be part of their thought process and not spoken aloud. They want to know how big the woods are, what kind of dog is running, and how fast the is dog moving. In their rush to answer the question they ignore the obvious and create unnecessary layers of complexity that do nothing to help them solve the riddle.

The closing message here is the same mantra you were taught when you were very young and started to venture out into the word: STOP, LOOK, and LISTEN. Children are told to do this whenever they cross a street. STOP, LOOK, and LISTEN should also be your watchwords when you are faced with a challenge. Don't start solving the problem before you have all of the available facts and understand the problem at hand.

Putting It All Together

Your Work Ethic

At the end of the day, it's a wonderful feeling to be able to say, "Yes, I did make a difference."

Interactions with Others

We each have the daily opportunity to improve our interpersonal relationships with our co-workers.

Teamwork

It is truly amazing what a committed team is capable of accomplishing. It is equally amazing how much damage a dysfunctional team can cause.

Creativity

While there are many wrong answers to any given problem, there is rarely only one right answer, so stretch beyond your grasp to lengthen your reach.

Thinking Outside of the Box

Situational awareness, coupled with individual preparedness and calculated risk taking, will lead you to new horizons.

The Five Building Blocks of Success—A Review

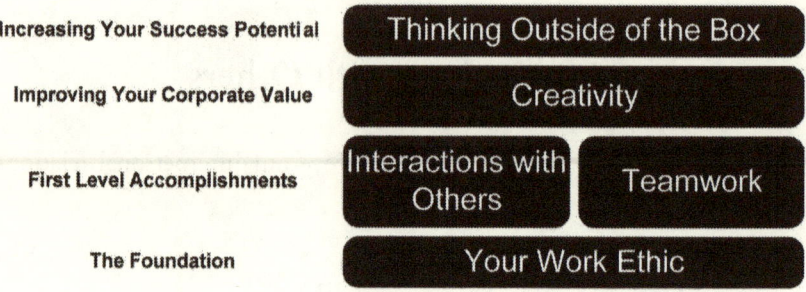

Increasing Your Success Potential	Thinking Outside of the Box
Improving Your Corporate Value	Creativity
First Level Accomplishments	Interactions with Others / Teamwork
The Foundation	Your Work Ethic

Like the bricks in a wall, the Five Building Blocks of Success are all interdependent upon each other for strength and stability. As the individual pursues continuous development in their skills and abilities, they will improve their value to the enterprise.

Your Work Ethic

When you begin your career, it is easy to be excited about the future and the opportunities that, with hope, lie ahead. Over time, however, things do have a tendency to change. The job gets difficult, or you have a boss who makes going to work a less-than-pleasant experience. You have some trouble with your social life, and your performance on the job suffers as a result. Or, you get married, buy a house, maybe have children, but in any event, you become burdened with an ever-increasing amount of external responsibilities that vie for your attention. In other words, it is easy to get distracted from the task at hand.

You don't have to be an automaton or a mindless drone to achieve success. You do, however, have to put forth a genuine effort if success is truly a goal.

I said before that some people seem to simply fall into the lap of success. Whether it is due to their birthright or plain old fashion luck, good things always happen to a select few, despite their lack of effort. Most of us, though, don't find ourselves in these situations. Most of us have to reap our rewards in amounts directly proportional to the effort we have put forth.

Getting up in the morning and looking forward to going to work is a great feeling, as is getting back home at the end of the day knowing that you have made a genuine contribution on behalf of your company. Most people take pride in a job well done. But it does not just happen. A job well done is the result of a focused, dedicated, and committed effort.

For most of us, there is a pretty direct correlation between the effort we put forth and the rewards we reap. I have witnessed people who contribute very little complain about their lack of progress—lack of raises, promotions, new job opportunities—yet fail to see that their failure has been predetermined by their lack of effort. I have also witnessed people who do work hard, but achieve only modest success. They also have not received the large raises they hoped for, or the promotions they longed for. This apparent dichotomy—working hard but receiving little in return—is explained by the fact that success requires other components beyond plain, old-fashioned hard work and dedicated effort.

Businesses need future leaders at all levels of the organization. The next generation of leadership is what helps ensure the continuation of the enterprise. But businesses also need people to fulfill a variety of positions throughout their organizations. So hard workers who do a very good job at what they do often won't grow within their organization if they don't exhibit the other components of success that we have explored in this book. They may receive some of what they have been looking for—reasonable raises, some recognition for their contributions—but they never seem to reach the level of success they hoped to achieve when they started on the journey we call their career.

Interactions with Others

In almost every assignment and position you could hold within an organization you need to work with co-workers. They may be peers in the same department, or individuals in another department who send you information or to whom you send information. In addition to peers, you will work with supervisors and managers who tell you what to do, as well as members of levels beneath yours who may be relying on you to tell them what to do. Further—depending upon the role you are fulfilling—you may interact with multiple contacts outside the company including representatives from customers and/or suppliers.

In order to be successful, an employee must be seen as a positive contributor to the organization by the members of the organization. If all people see is a fellow employee who cannot—for whatever reasons—get along with other people, that person, even if recognized as a hard worker, will rarely, if ever, be promoted into a higher position or given additional responsibilities, especially if interaction with others is required.

People thrive in positive environments. A positive and friendly working environment results in a self-sustaining pool of energy that people within the environment can draw from. The interpersonal relationships that develop can be a catalyst for further individual and group development.

It really does not cost anything to treat others with respect and kindness, and this is the type of investment that can reap huge dividends.

Teamwork

Sometime during your career you will be part of a team that has been assigned to accomplish a specific goal. The team that can leverage the collective efforts of the individuals that comprise the team is generally successful in its endeavors. The team that is dysfunctional most likely fails, or generates only mediocre results.

Being on a team is different from carrying out your normal every-day functions of your job. Jobs—positions and their accompanying responsibilities—tend to be ongoing. Though the tasks performed may be repetitive in nature, the job goes on from day to day. The person fulfilling the role has a reasonable expectation that, short of quitting or being fired, his or her employment in that position will go on into the future.

Being on a team, however, is typically different because there is a time limit imposed on its existence. Thus the duration of the existence of the team correlates to the value of its members being able to work together effectively.

A sort-duration team that exists for a couple of hours to develop the theme for the office picnic does not necessarily rely on the strength of the interpersonal relationships among its team members as a critical success factor. The success of a long-duration team—the team charged with coming up with next year's new product offerings—however, is very dependent upon the ebb and flow of the interpersonal relationships of its team members. If there is constant infighting, little progress is made. If, on the other hand, all energies are focused and directed towards a successful outcome, the chances for success are increased dramatically.

All members of the team have an obligation to themselves, the other team members, and the organization for which they work to put forth their best effort possible. The benefits to be derived from the collective efforts of a focused, high-energy team can be significant, and group behavior that encourages a positive team environment should be stressed and encouraged.

Creativity

The only thing constant in today's hectic working environment is that the rate of change is increasing. What used to take years to develop can now be accomplished in months, weeks, or even days in many of the industries that are currently producing the goods and/or services that we demand. Businesses that fail to heed the consumer cry for new and different products and/or services frequently find that they are being outclassed by their competition—and, as a direct result, they either close up shop, or are acquired by larger, stronger companies.

True or false: Being able to look into the future and project what the changing business landscape will look like is the purview of CEOs, senior executives, and those in business development roles. My answer to this question: false.

Your particular role may not come with the formal responsibility of gazing into a crystal ball, but you should know that truly successful people do tend to spend some time thinking about the future. They look for ways to improve what they are doing. This might be the development and application of new software, the elimination of unnecessary and unproductive steps, or re-engineering a process to account for changing consumer tastes. At other times improvement steps might follow the Japanese concept of *Kaizen*, where small, incremental improvements on a daily or weekly basis accumulate and result in significant changes when viewed over time. Or, someone may decide to process map a particular task to uncover duplication in effort, or unnecessary steps. And then there is the urban legend example of simply stopping to issue a particular report—that might be classified as archaic—to see if anyone complains.

Creativity is a combination of inspiration and perspiration. Spend some time thinking about how improvements can be identified and implemented. Successful people dedicate themselves to continuous personal improvement. Successful people also apply this same philosophy to the role they fulfill within an organization.

Thinking Outside of the Box

What if we do this, or do that? How many times have "what if" questions been asked? And how many times have they simply been rejected because "we tried that before" or "we don't do things that way around here"?

Every single policy, procedure, technique, and method does not need to be re-examined each and every day. Sometimes the way we do things is the best way, or at least adequate for the situation. Making changes for the sake of making changes is not necessarily a good idea. If the new way is more expensive and ultimately costs the company more money—thereby making the enterprise less profitable—it probably does not make sense to adopt the new idea.

Some people confuse the concept of thinking outside of the box with the situation described in the paragraph above. We said previously that thinking outside of the box is the concept of using old answers in new ways. Adopting a procedure or technique that is used in one application for another application is what we are describing. Sometimes this happens in response to a question such as, "So how do we solve this problem?" At other times it is the spontaneous thought proceeded by a "what if" question.

Truly successful people keep their eyes, ears, and minds open. They don't limit their view of the world based solely upon convention or tried-and-true methods. When faced with a challenge, they seek to understand the situation before jumping to any conclusions. Viewing each and every challenge with a fresh, unbiased perspective aids in stimulating outside of the box thinking and could lead to some interesting solutions.

We used the phrase "situational awareness" in the beginning of this section when we offered a summary sentence to describe outside of the box thinking. Situational awareness is the state of being aware of what is going on around you. By tuning in to your business environment—being aware of the various issues that comprise your business world—you will be able to proactively take advantage of opportunities and anticipate situations where problems and challenges may develop. In other words, you do not have to wait for an issue to arise before you tune in to your own situational awareness.

It is said that that luck favors the prepared mind. If you have situational awareness and have prepared yourself from an abilities/skill set point of view, you will be prepared when things start to happen around you. If an opportunity arises—or a problem or a challenge—you will find that you are able to react positively—and maybe even proactively—in developing a course of action that will benefit you and those you represent. Unprepared people call this luck. Prepared people know that productive reactions to situations like these can help get them a step or two farther along on the road to success.

Future challenges

Sooner or later in our careers almost all of us encounter potential threats to our continued employment. Sometimes these threats are external in nature. Your company encounters some tough times with sales lagging and profitability falling. All of a sudden, you are faced with the prospect of losing your job due to the corporate—division, department, or work group—decision to downsize. Or, your company either acquires another company, or your company is acquired. Once again, downsizing is one of the chief tactics used to generate cost reductions. Or, an organization change brings in a new boss who has plans to populate his department with his own people. Then again, the new boss may just be a jerk who is out to make everyone's life miserable. In all of these cases, you could lose your job.

At other times, the imminent threat of loss of employment has become a self-fulfilling destiny brought about by actions you did or did not take. For any variety of reasons you may have lost focus and stopped trying to do your best. Your performance level decreased and, all of a sudden, someone in authority has declared you deadwood. Before you know it, you are called on the carpet and given your exit package—assuming, of course, that they offer you an exit package. They could just terminate your employment.

External Threats to Your Continued Employment

Few of us have the luxury of guaranteed employment. There are so many variables in play at any one time that often, even though we think we have our bases covered, something unexpected happens and we find ourselves at risk.

In spite of this, we can do things to help insulate ourselves in the event the unforeseen starts to occur. In most cases, when companies downsize, decisions about who to let go are influenced by prior performance. If you have established yourself as a can-do, will-do, dynamic performer, you stand a better chance of being kept on board than someone who is just an average performer. Conversely, if you do just enough to get by, get used to the fact that you will probably be among the first to go if the need for downsizing ever arises.

So to a degree, while you cannot guarantee your future employment with any one particular company, your performance level does have a direct bearing when push comes to shove and your employer starts shoving people out of the door. The smart employer will, obviously, keep the best performers.

Self-Generated Threats
Today is the First Day in the Rest of Your Career

You cannot undo that which has been done. If you have been a lackluster performer up to and including today, there is no time like the present to sit back, take stock of your abilities, assess your skill set, and dedicate yourself to improving your performance levels.

I assume that most people who are reading this book are genuinely interested in continued self-improvement. In this regard, taking stock of your abilities and skill set is a very productive step in that continued development. You must know your starting point in order to determine your destination.

As we said several times throughout this book, everyone has his or her own definition of the word success. Not everyone wants to be the CEO, nor does everyone want to be the subject matter expert in trans-continental logistics. As you sit back and assess your career aspirations, be honest in your appraisal of your abilities. If you lack something, recognize it and seek out the help and/or information that will enable you to overcome this shortcoming. If you have what you need now, imagine yourself in the next level within your organization and reassess your abilities and skill set based upon the requirements of that position. If you need to hone a skill, or add a skill, and you aspire to that position, then by all means learn what you need to learn. When the position becomes open, you will be that much more attractive to whoever is making the placement decision.

Success doesn't just happen. If you take this as a given, you recognize that the only person truly controlling your chances for success is you. You have the power to demonstrate the depth and quality of your skills to others. You also have the power to simply sit back and expect success to come knocking at your door. You have to decide which path you want to follow.

Review checklist

The following milestones are offered as reminders of what a successful person should want to accomplish relative to each of the five building blocks of success:

- Your Work Ethic
    - o Strive to obtain a performance rating of *excellent* or *superior*.
    - o Demonstrate a thorough understanding of your responsibilities.
    - o Demonstrate your understanding of how your efforts interact with and contribute to the overall effort of your department or work group.
    - o Invest the hours necessary to be successful.
    - o Seek out continuous developmental and skill set improvement opportunities.
- Interactions with Others
    - o Treat others as you wish to be treated.
    - o Be fair, firm, and friendly in your dealings with your co-workers.
    - o Conduct yourself with dignity.
    - o Be honest and trustworthy in all of your interactions.
- Teamwork
    - o Understand the purpose and goal(s) of your team.
    - o Understand your role as a team member.
    - o Aid your team members in accomplishing their portion of the assignment when feasible and appropriate.
- Creativity
    - o Do not impose self-generated limits to a challenge or opportunity.
    - o Be positive in word, spirit, and deed during blue-sky sessions.
    - o Do not be afraid to contribute "what if" suggestions.
    - o Do not let past failures keep you from forming new ideas.
- Thinking Outside of the Box
    - o Do not impose self-generated limits to a challenge or opportunity.
    - o Stop, look, and listen before you embark upon a search for a solution.
    - o Use colleagues and peers as sounding boards for new ideas.

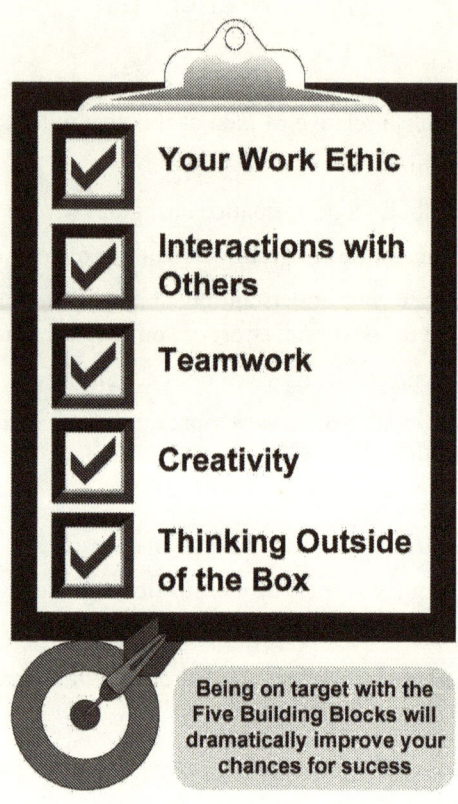

Career Planning Guide

You can use the following worksheets to assist you in developing your own personal growth strategy for each of the five building blocks of success.

LONG-TERM GOALS

Current position _____

Current income _____

Role/responsibility—Where do you see yourself:

In Five Years _____

By mid-career _____

By end of career _____

Income—What do you envision your income level:

In five years _____

By mid-career _____

By end of career _____

Education/skill set—What developmental steps must you take:

In five years _____

By mid-career _____

By end of career _____

Mobility—Would you relocate in order to accomplish your goals?

Domestically _____

Internationally _____

YOUR WORK ETHIC

Keeping your personal long-term goals in mind, answer the following questions:

What is your current performance rating (e.g., average, above average)?

_____

What area(s) did your immediate supervisor—or whoever gave you your most recent performance review—tell you that you need to improve?

1. _____

2. _____

3. _____

4. _____

5. _____

What specific steps have you taken to improve in those areas identified as needing attention?

1. _____

2. _____

3. _____

4. _____

5. _____

What additional training and/or skill set expansion will you need to be able to accomplish your five-year role/responsibility goal, and what steps are you taking to ensure that you accomplish them?

_____

_____

_____

_____

_____

_____

_____

_____

What additional training and/or skill set expansion will you need to be able to accomplish your mid-career role/responsibility goal and what steps are you taking to ensure that you accomplish them?

_____

_____

_____

_____

_____

_____

What additional training and/or skill set expansion will you need to be able to accomplish your end-of-career role/responsibility goal and what steps are you taking to ensure that you accomplish them?

_____

_____

_____

_____

_____

_____

_____

Will you be able to accomplish your role/responsibility and income goals at the same company in which you are currently employed, and, if not, what else will you need to do in order to accomplish your end-of-career goals?

_____

_____

_____

_____

_____

_____

_____

INTERACTIONS WITH OTHERS

Being able to effectively interact with others is a key component of success, especially in a large organization. In this regard, perform an honest self-appraisal ranking of your abilities in the following areas, all of which help drive effective interactions with others:

Poor   Excellent

- Communication skills—oral...

- Communications skills—written ....

- Organization skills ....

- Friendliness in current interactions ....

- Honesty in current interactions...................................

- Appearance...

- Flexibility...

- Ability to deal with difficult people.............................

- Ability to control temper ....

- Level of your social skills...

- Your overall assessment of
  your interpersonal skills ....

What courses, classes, and/or seminars have you taken to improve your interpersonal skills?

_____

_____

_____

_____

_____

_____

Have you ever received a performance appraisal in which it was suggested that you improve your interpersonal skills? If you have, what aspects of your interpersonal skills were referenced and what improvement steps were suggested?

_____

_____

_____

_____

_____

_____

_____

Did you complete any training or seek out any other source of personal development to improve your interpersonal skill set and, if you did, what did you accomplish?

_____

_____

_____

_____

TEAMWORK

It is difficult to imagine that a person can have poor interpersonal skills, yet be able to function well as a member of a team. This section will help you assess your ability to function well as a team member.

Are you currently part of a team and, if so, in what capacity (e.g., leader, facilitator, contributor, support):

_____

_____

_____

_____

_____

If you are not part of a team, is it because the opportunity has never been presented to you, or is it because you have not been selected to participate?

_____

_____

_____

_____

_____

_____

_____

If you were not selected, was it because of a shortcoming in your interpersonal skill set and, if so, what steps are you taking to overcome these shortcomings?

_____

_____

_____

_____

_____

_____

_____

CREATIVITY

Creativity per se cannot be taught. One can be exposed to different concepts regarding creativity and how to get the juices flowing, but, at the core, some people are just more creative than other people. In fact, some people are so rigid in their thinking and convictions that they are unable to be creative, especially in areas or on topics that contradict their preconceived notions.

By way of an example—the business you are currently in—we will explore an outline that should help the creative juices flow.

What mix of goods and/or services does your current company provide to its customers?

_____

_____

_____

_____

_____

_____

_____

_____

_____

Who are your primary and secondary customers (e.g., what types of people or organizations use your good and/or services)?

_____

_____

_____

_____

_____

_____

What are the strengths and weaknesses of your organization in terms of its goods and/or services as perceived by your customers?

_____

_____

_____

_____

_____

_____

Now, assume that you leave your employer and become the CEO of one of your competitors and that you have a copy of the answers to the three previous questions. What would you do to compete effectively against your previous employer (how would you use its strategy and positioning in the market as levers to help you compete)?

_____

_____

_____

_____

_____

_____

_____

_____

_____

_____

_____

_____

_____

_____

_____

_____

Review your last answer and, if it boils down to simply being better, faster, and/or cheaper than your previous employer, rethink your strategy based upon a completely new approach (e.g., changing consumer perceptions, adding new goods and/or services, et cetera).

_____

_____

_____

_____

_____

_____

_____

_____

_____

_____

_____

_____

_____

_____

_____

_____

_____

_____

_____

Project yourself ten years into the future and assume that technology and consumer tastes, wants, and needs—real and/or perceived—will change. As the
CEO, how will you position your business to proactively take advantage of these
opportunities?

_____

_____

_____

_____

_____

_____

_____

_____

_____

_____

_____

_____

_____

_____

_____

_____

_____

_____

THINKING OUTSIDE OF THE BOX

This exercise will help you to develop outside of the box thinking.

Describe a problem that you—or your team, department, division, or company—is currently facing.

_____

_____

_____

_____

_____

_____

_____

_____

_____

_____

_____

_____

_____

_____

_____

_____

_____

_____

_____

Limiting your thought process to available resources—headcount, technology, and/or funding—describe three possible solutions to overcome the problem facing you.

1. _____

_____

_____

2. _____

_____

_____

3. _____

_____

_____

Now, assume that you have unlimited resources available. How would your answers to the previous question change?

1. _____

_____

_____

2. _____

_____

_____

3. _____

_____

_____

Discuss this exercise with three peers in your organization and, without sharing your answers with them, ask them to provide their own solutions to the problem at hand. How did their solutions differ from your solutions and why did they differ?

1. _____

_____

_____

_____

_____

2. _____

_____

_____

_____

_____

3. _____

_____

_____

_____

_____

About the Author

David A. Bragen is the author of the award-winning business book *A Beginner's Guide to a Successful Career* and *Corporate Characters—Understanding the Personalities of Your Co-Workers* (available online at Amazon.com and Booksamillion.com) and is the founder and president of DAVEN Consulting, Inc., a firm dedicated to helping publishers make cost effective supply chain supplier selections. In his career, David has held a number of senior management positions with R.R. Donnelley, North American Directory Corporation, Quebecor Printing Inc., and, most recently, Quebecor World, then the largest commercial printer in the world. As a division president for Quebecor World, David's profit-and-loss (P&L) responsibilities included ten manufacturing facilities, a national sales force, a team of more than 2,400 employees, as well as top line revenues of $400,000,000.

David holds both a BBA and MBA from Loyola University in Chicago, Illinois. He resides in Wheaton, Illinois, with his wife and two children. He enjoys hunting, golf, woodworking, and writing.

978-0-595-43359-9
0-595-43359-6